The Nightingale Sings Alone

By R.H. Fowler

R.H. Fowler

Copyright © 2016 by Robert H. Fowler
All rights reserved. This book or any portion thereof
may not be reproduced or used in any manner whatsoever
without the express written permission of the publisher
except for the use of brief quotations in a book review. For all
inquiries, email rhfowlerwriter@gmail.com

Printed in the United States of America

First Printing, 2016

ISBN: 978-1-329-76591-7

The Nightingale Sings Alone

Dedication

This book is dedicated
To anyone
Who has ever lost themselves
Over love
Only to find themselves
Hurt,
And out of place
In life.
This is for anyone
Who has struggled
Violently
With rejection,
And for anyone
That will face off
With the cruel
Concept.
This is for all of us,
Hurting, or healing.

I hope these words
Make you feel,
And make you
Appreciate love
And loss
As two wings
Of the same
Bird.

Here's to hoping.

R.H. Fowler

The Nightingale
Sings Alone

By R.H. Fowler

Edited by J.D. Wallace

No. 1

The nightingale sings
A rapturous tune
Outside of my window-sill,
But the only sound
I hear
Is the sharp
Song of our
Twisted howling
At each other.
Oh,
How delightful
The echoing can be.

R.H. Fowler

No. 2

There is no calm
In the night.
That is a great lie we are told.
No, for you see
The darkness
Holds many
Vicious secrets
Closely,
Providing only
An illusion of safety
From Mother Nature's
Wrath.

The Nightingale Sings Alone

No. 3

Walk with me
Into the trenches
Of my mind,
My beloved,
You'll find a quietness
There
Far more enveloping
Than any sound
Could hope
To possibly be.

R.H. Fowler

No. 4

Maybe the stars
Are just as hopeless
As we sometimes can be,
And turn to the
Magnificent beauty
Of our radiant
Blue world
When everything else
In this vastly cold,
Vastly uninviting universe
Seems lost.

The Nightingale Sings Alone

No. 5

Believe your brain,
It's usually right,
For hearts get maimed
And we lose sight.

R.H. Fowler

No. 6

You must sprint away
From my love
This very instant.
It is not safe to
Stand so close
To such
Concentrated fury,
Especially when that
Fury
Reeks of
Whiskey & wine.

The Nightingale Sings Alone

No. 7

We go to war with
Our thoughts,
Debating constantly,
"What's fair, what's not?"
What we wished
We could've changed
In the past.

These musings consume us.

We forget that
Through it all--
The beauty
Of life, and living
Is in being able
To experience
Such pain,
And reflect on it
With gallons of
Grace, joy,
And thoughtfulness,
As we know
Great human-beings can.

R.H. Fowler

No. 8

Sanity was never a
Strong suit of mine,
My dear.
It is evident
In the way
I love
So
Haphazard
And
Helplessly.

The Nightingale Sings Alone

No. 9

The rub of it all
Is that we are
One
With the chaos
We create.
Trying to find
The difference
Between that
Maddening place,
And love?
That is the goal
We all wish to
Achieve,
I suppose,
As we cling
To this vision
That one is
Far different
Than the other.

R.H. Fowler

No. 10

Walking out into
The night,
Deprived,
Alone again,
Always searching
Yet staying stationary
In the looming darkness—
No street lamps in sight
To brighten my melancholy.
What a beautiful, quiet space
This magical silence is.

The Nightingale Sings Alone

No. 11

Beware how
Loudly
Your heart beats
When potential
Falsehoods & fakeries
Appear.
The drumming in your chest
Is able
To tell the difference
Between good
And bad
Intentions.
It is
Too pure for
The nonsensical
Notion that it won't catch on
To wickedness when it
Rears its horrid horns.

No, for you see,
Our wandering mind
Is often to blame
For trapping
Our beating love
In chaotic realms.

R.H. Fowler

No. 12

Love begins
When you accept
The admirably odd notion
That someone
Could possibly
Find redemption
Within your graveyard
Of faults and failures.

You must always
Love
Yourself
First.

The Nightingale Sings Alone

No. 13

We drive ourselves
To the brink
Of destruction
For our glistening goals—
But is it not really
All
For the type of
Love
And validation
We value
So vehemently?

R.H. Fowler

No. 14

I wouldn't ask
You
To partake
In my perpetual madness,
But at the end
Of the day,
Your presence
Is the only thing
That seems to
Quell
The brutish beast.

So won't you
Please sing me
Your lullaby
Tonight?

The Nightingale Sings Alone

No. 15

I look for rest,
Futilely fighting against
The ocean's strong currents,
Trying not to get
Swept out to sea,
And to my death.
The waves constantly shift,
Throwing me off course
From any semblance
Of normality...
But maybe the lack
Of consistency
Is my
Natural state
Of being.
And the waves
Of the ocean
Are my
Dear
Brothers.

R.H. Fowler

No. 16

Be wary of those
Who arise
From the cruel ashes
Of life's roaring volcano.
Playing carelessly
With their fractured heart
Will only leave you
Burnt beyond compare.

The Nightingale Sings Alone

No. 17

We live day to day
And do the best
We can
To keep darkness out
Of our minds,
And out
Of our lives.
Not because we
Fear angels and demons,
I think it's more of a
Tragic fear.
It is
The frightening feeling
That we are only memories,
And grains of dust,
And the feelings
We left behind
In the people we loved
On this earth.

We want those feelings
To be cherished.
So we try to do well
By them,
And do the best
We can
To keep darkness out
Of our lives.

R.H. Fowler

No. 18

We punish ourselves
For not loving
Correctly,
And push each other
Away when we love
Too
Hard.
What an unbelievably cruel species
We have become.

The Nightingale Sings Alone

No. 19

Is it really my time
To stare down the
Loveless,
Cold-steel barrel
Of life's expectations?
Run with me,
My love,
We can board the
Last train
To oblivion
If we sprint
Fast enough
Through this crowd
Of masked-strangers.

R.H. Fowler

No. 20

The crippling blow
Was struck
Long before
You arrived.

You were simply
The only one
Who could
Revive me
After the battle
Was over.

The Nightingale Sings Alone

No. 21

The fire that raged
In her soul
Was one born
Out of gut-wrenching
Sadness.
What a haunting
Blaze it was,
So desperate
For water
As it consumed
Everything in its
Path.

R.H. Fowler

No. 22

Be prepared
To fall
Off of this tight-rope
With me,
My dear,
I never claimed
To have
Any sort
Of balance
In the
First place.

The Nightingale Sings Alone

No. 23

Memories of you
Cling to my mind
Like a shadow
At dusk.
The only way
To shake the
Stifling sadness
Is to wait for night,
The darkness of things
Swallowing up
All bitter feelings,
Sweeping them
Into distant corners
Of nothingness
While I watch the stars above.

R.H. Fowler

No. 24

Leave me to
My self-destruction.
It is much prettier
At sunset
When you know
It could be
Your last time
Feeling its warmth.

The Nightingale Sings Alone

No. 25

A good lie
Is often
The only
Comfortable song
We can hear
In most
Instances of pain.
We might
As well
Be blissfully
Ignorant,
Drunk off of
Life,
As they say.

R.H. Fowler

No. 26

I have yet to really
Touch life,
Fingers crossed,
Bones broken from the pressure,
I stir in a cage
Of my own thoughts.
The open door
Creaking violently,
Illuminating an exit
I will never pay
Attention to
Because the bright
Light of my ego
Refuses to let me
See the change I need
Over the comfort I desire.
I will instead
Forever debate
My great escape
To an audience
That will always
Applaud
The wrong decision.

The Nightingale Sings Alone

No. 27

We were much more
Than a love affair
Gone awry.
We were the universe
Itself
Trying to be
Felt,
Trying to be
Understood.

Too bad the cosmos
Were never there
For us to comprehend.

R.H. Fowler

No. 28

The worst part
Of all this mangled
Mess,
Was that I tortured
Myself with the notion
That you really
Gave a damn
About a future
With me.

The Nightingale Sings Alone

No. 29

I paint my
Masterpieces
With broad strokes
Of the brush,
Every sharp
Detail
Marked with
Broken pieces
Of me,
And thoughts
Of you.

R.H. Fowler

No. 30

Many hearts will be
Tortured
By your love,
But that is fine,
Because real
Experience
Does not
Freely abound
In our plastic,
Parasitic reality.

The Nightingale Sings Alone

No. 31

I have
Been alone
For so long
That I
Find myself
Fearful
Of my own
Shadow,
Praying
For it
To fade
Into the nighttime
That surrounds
Me.

R.H. Fowler

No. 32

If only
Love
Didn't
Burn
Everything
It touched
To ash,
Then maybe
We would all
Enjoy the light
And warmth
The inferno itself
Creates.

The Nightingale Sings Alone

No. 33

I'd love
To bask
In the light
Your smile
Provides,
But I am
Too busy
Foolishly
Searching
For
Illumination
In the darkness
Of my own
Twisted soul.

R.H. Fowler

No. 34

She
Seemed
To have
The eyes
Of an eagle,
The way she
Made quick work
Of her prey.
What a wondrous
Way to go,
Amidst the wings
Of perfection,
Enamored,
Then destroyed
In a flash.

The Nightingale Sings Alone

No. 35

It is horribly
Tragic,
But I feel
As if
My friends,
My family,
Those who
Truly love me,
Love me far more
Than I do myself
Sometimes.
There is a beauty
In that
Which makes
Me look for the goodness
And grace
They see in my eyes,
And truly admire it
In my own self.

I wish that feeling
Would always last,
But humans are
Quite forgetful.

R.H. Fowler

No. 36

Forgive me
For worshiping
At the altar
Of your faults,
But it is
The only
Religion
That I know,
And that I know
To be true,
As all faults
Unearth the most subtle
Of revelations
Giving us insight…

If only for the moment.

The Nightingale Sings Alone

No. 37

Do not let my
Crude, chaotic nature
Deceive you.
There is certainly
A heart in my
Chest,
And love
In my soul.
Separating
Them all
However
Is far more
Challenging
Than I could
Even hope.

R.H. Fowler

No. 38

The further we
Trace our footsteps
Away
From love's embrace,
The less we
Recognize
What it
Looks like
When we
Stumble
Upon
The creature
In the wilderness
Of our own hearts.

The Nightingale Sings Alone

No. 39

My heart
Was never
For sale.
It was simply
Stolen in the night,
Under the lovely lights
Of the starry
Heavens above
By you and your
Yearning
For more.

R.H. Fowler

No. 40

I have let myself
Writhe
In agony
And loneliness
So much,
That it's
No wonder
Why
You just
Couldn't
Fucking
Bear
To stay
A moment
Longer.
You were insane for
Staying
So long.

Ha, ha!

Drunken fools
Are maddening.

The Nightingale Sings Alone

No. 41

I loved the way
Her words used
To singe me so.
I guess that's why
I can't help but
Romance this
Bottle of gin,
In hopes that a
Similar flame
Ignites
My spirit
Once more.

R.H. Fowler

No. 42

Must we spend our lives
Journeying from
Milestone to milestone?
Or is the joke on us
Who revel in the decadence
Of doing nothing?

The Nightingale Sings Alone

No. 43

I guess I am
In love with
Loneliness,
It is the fire
In my stomach,
The blaze
That too much
Scotch helps
Spread amongst
The dying leaves
That wish to burn
In my soul.

I guess I am
In love with
Loneliness,
But I think
Loneliness
Is getting
Sick of me.

I know I'm
Getting sick
Of her nagging.

R.H. Fowler

No. 44

Is it really just
A choice of
Which path
To take in life?
Or should we
Be so bold
As to slog
Through
The muck,
Building our
Way
Brick by brick
To a paradise
We create ourselves?

The Nightingale Sings Alone

No. 45

There is a fragile veil
That separates
Dusk and dawn
From the night.
We must
Never forget
This thin line
My love,
But try to find
Beauty
In the stars that are
Visible
During the twilight
Hours of
Our days
Together.

R.H. Fowler

No. 46

I know what it feels like
To not understand.
To feel like everything I've known
Is not
What I know it to be.
You are not solitary
In your madness.
The clouds are thick,
But we are all
With you,
Reaching out
In the darkness,
Waiting for the
Inevitable
Light of the sun.

The Nightingale Sings Alone

No. 47

Never ruin
Yourself
With love,
Embrace
Its rising
Tide,
And leave it be
In the morning.
At least
You won't
Be lost
In the ocean
Of the damned
When it tries to
Lure you
To sea.

R.H. Fowler

No. 48

The world is
Cruel and cold,
But your
Embrace
Was heat
And warmth.
It is only right
For me to be
Made of ice,
Unable to
Enjoy such
Radiant affection.

The Nightingale Sings Alone

No. 49

We can never
Truly wear
Our heart
On our sleeves.
Not in this
Jumbled, judgmental
World.
It's a shame,
Because
Everybody's
Struggle
Is so vastly
Different,
And yet we
Are all one
And the same
In our despair.

R.H. Fowler

No. 50

If my dreams
Are infinite,
Then why do they
Cling
To visions
Of your beauty?
It's as if our courtship
Was doomed
To draw me as close
To your spirit
As a wino clutching
His bottle
Of burning
Memories.
How hypnotizing
The dying embers
Become with each sip.
Dancing in a
Sea of malt,
Submerging
And drenching
Those infernal
Thoughts of you...
At least for
The night,
Anyway.

The Nightingale Sings Alone

No. 51

We unlock our hearts
For those that we think
Do not need a key,
We simply give
Them a pass.
All the while,
They pocket our
Finery, robbing us
Blind,
Leaving
Us fractured
From the very
Thought
Of opening
The door again.

R.H. Fowler

No. 52

The way
I looked
At her
Was the way
I wish I could
Look at all of
The beautiful
Things
I neglect
In this wondrous
World.

The Nightingale Sings Alone

No. 53

We stride with
Our long steps,
Cloaking the pain
Felt
From each
Shocking thud
Of the foot.

One after the
Other,
Plodding
Towards nowhere,
With nothing
On this desert
Road
Except for me,
And that
Endless horizon
I have yet
To embrace
The majesty of.

R.H. Fowler

No. 54

Tie me to
Your battered
Soul
And let me
Trace those scars
With my ravaged
Fingertips.

The Nightingale Sings Alone

No. 55

If only you
Could see
How I destroy
My brain
With thoughts
Of every sentence
You've said
To me,
I undoubtedly
Know then
That you would
Think twice
About how
You use
Those
Words
You so
Cleverly
Twist and bend.

R.H. Fowler

No. 56

We must melt
Into this
Frenzy of
Filth
And vile
Lust
When we
Embrace,
Because nothing
This good
Can be anything
But wrong
In the eyes
Of the less
Fortunate.

The Nightingale Sings Alone

No. 57

It was our mistake
To love so recklessly.
I can only hope
I am not so foolish
Again, my dear,
But the heart
And the brain
Are in separate
Places
For a reason.

R.H. Fowler

No. 58

We loved so deeply
Death himself
Almost
Forgot us.
But "almost"
Is a word
Never found
In fairytale
Endings.

The Nightingale Sings Alone

No. 59

We were so distant
I never thought
A connection
Possible.
Your gaze
So luminous
I never thought
Of looking directly
At your beauty.
But, sometimes,
We must
Sail towards the
Light,
Just to see
What lays beyond
That sublime
Sunset.

R.H. Fowler

No. 60

Is life itself
Not poetry?
The way it
Twists and turns
The magnificent
Into the horrid
And vice versa?
The way it
Leaves you
Dumbfounded
From the beauty
Of how painfully
Brilliant
The love...
And the loss
Can be?

It is all poetry
To me.

The Nightingale Sings Alone

No. 61

Do not be afraid
Of the monsters
That rise in
The dark mire
Of your mind,
For you see,
They are just as
Fearful
As you are.

Shall we turn
The lights on?

R.H. Fowler

No. 62

We all want
A great romance,
One Cleopatra
And Marc Antony
Themselves
Would envy.
The problem is that
There are only
Two ways
In which that fantasy
Could end.
So what shall we choose,
My dear?
The sword or
The snake?

The Nightingale Sings Alone

The End

I want to thank you all
For reading my words.
I am nothing without them,
And nothing without
The people who inspire me
To continue.

I love you all.

R.H. Fowler

Follow RH Fowler for more poetry
And updates;

www.facebook.com/rhfpoet
www.twitter.com/rhfpoet
www.instagram.com/rhfpoet
www.tumblr.com/rhfpoet
snapchat: rhfpoet

Thank you all for reading!

55/1500